Carving Angels

Schiffer Publishing Ltd

77 Lower Valley Road, Atglen, PA 19310

Kelley Stadelman

Text written with and photography by
Douglas Congdon-Martin

Dedication

One special angel came to me about 5 years ago, Sandi Zickuhr. She taught me folk art style carving. The skills I have learned from her are the cornerstone of my success. These skills have guided me down a path which has made it possible to meet many wonderful people with whom I have shared the art of carving. Sandi, thank you for enriching all our lives through the art of carving.

Copyright © 1995 by Kelley Stadelman

Printed in China

ISBN: 0-88740-860-5

Book Design By Audrey L. Whiteside

Library of Congress Cataloging-in-Publication Data

Stadelman, Kelley.
      Carving angels / Kelley Stadelman; text written with and photography by Douglas Congdon-Martin.
          p.   cm.
      ISBN 0-88740-860-5 (pbk.)
      1. Wood-carving. 2. Wood-carved figurines.
   3. Angels in art. I. Congdon-Martin, Douglas.
   II. Title.
   TT199.7.S727
   736'.4--dc20   95-32236
                                                      CIP

Published by Schiffer Publishing, Ltd.
77 Lower Valley Road
Atglen, PA 19310
Please write for a free catalog.
This book may be purchased from the publisher.
Please include $2.95 postage.
Try your bookstore first.

We are interested in hearing from authors
with book ideas on related subjects.

Contents

Introduction

As a child I can remember having vivid images of my guardian angel and her angel friends. Those memories have influenced the projects in this book. These angels have their own distinct personality, but generally speaking they bubble with energy and have a wonderful sense of humor. I can remember imagining them buzzing around my companions' heads, stopping briefly to whisper messages of goodness into their ears. Then these winged bundles of giggles and song would be off to do other good deeds.

Now I realize that we are all angels at one time or another, being guided from above to do special works. Have you ever been caught in a situation that looked very bleak, and, by "chance," just the right person happened to arrive and change the situation for the better? Have you yourself ever been that person who changes a difficult or dangerous situation to one of security? I believe that much of what happens in our lives occurs by chance, but many of our actions are influenced by angels bearing messages from heaven.

I still cling to the whimsical images of angels from my past. As you carve these projects, I hope they will remind you to carve safely and protect you from harm.

If you have any questions about these projects regarding ready-to-carve sugar pine blanks, paint colors, or carving questions, please write or call.

Kelley Stadelman
P.O. Box 191
North Plains, OR 97133
(503) 647-0892

Angel Project Pattern

Carving the Angel

Cut the outline of the pattern on the bandsaw, using two inch sugar pine stock (1 1/2" actual thickness).

Draw around the body and head of the angel. The wings will be cut back quite a bit, so I don't draw them in until later.

Place a sheet of carbon or graphite paper between the pattern and the wood.

Ready for carving.

Score a line around the outside of the body.

A broader gouge can be used for more vigorous removal.

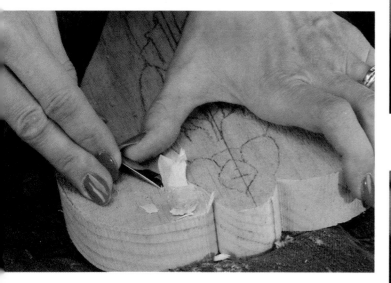

With a straight chisel cut back to the score line.

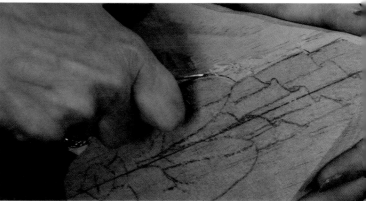

Rescore the line to deepen it...

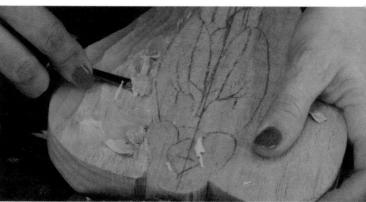

and continue reducing the wing.

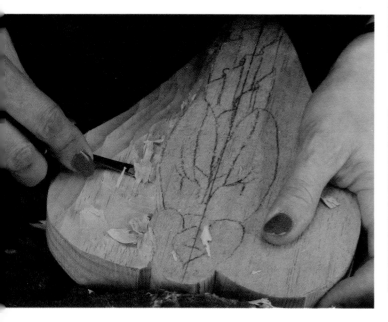

Reduce the wings with a gouge.

Where they the join, the surface of the wing should be at least 1/2 inch below the surface of the body.

Flatten the wings before rounding the edge.

One side done.

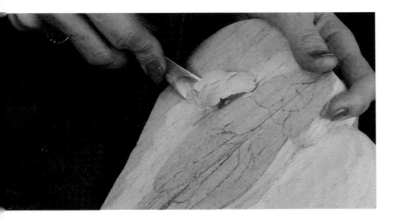

Continue on the other side.

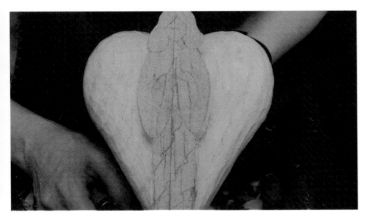

Both wings shaped.

Next I round off the edges of the head and body.

With the edges softened I can start cutting in details.

Redraw any lines that have been lost in carving.

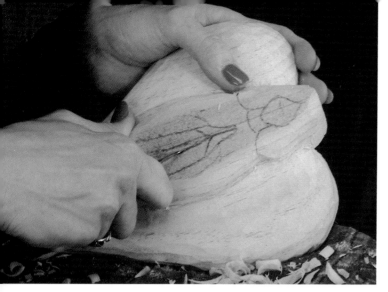

Score the bottom line of the sleeve.

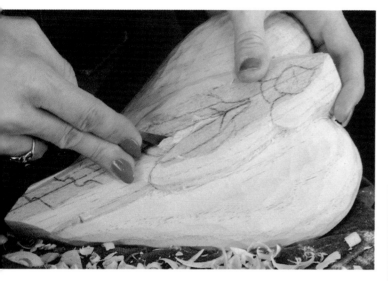

Cut back to the line from between the sleeves to drop the gown down.

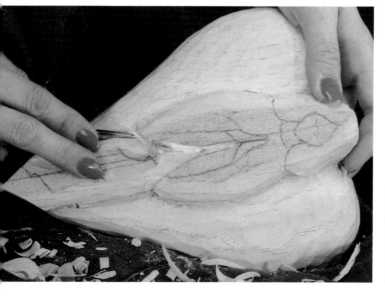

Continue around the bottom edge.

Deepen the score line...

and the space between the sleeves.

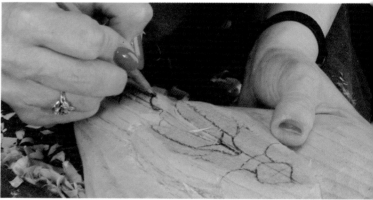

Redraw the lines.

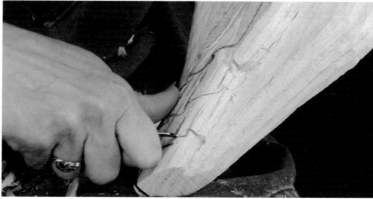

Score the bottom edge of the first tier of fabric.

Shape the lowest segment of the gown.

Finished.

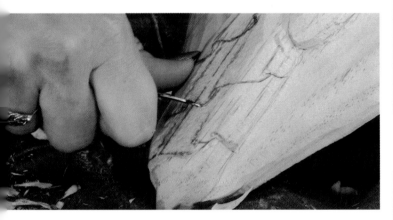

Score the bottom line of the next segment of the gown...

and shape the segment below it.

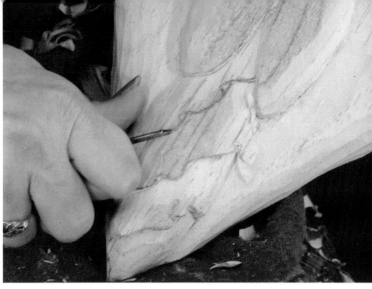

Continue up to the next segment, scoring the line...

and shaping the segment below it.

The layers are defined and ready for the linen folds.

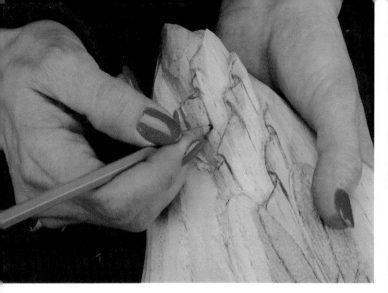

Redraw the fold lines.

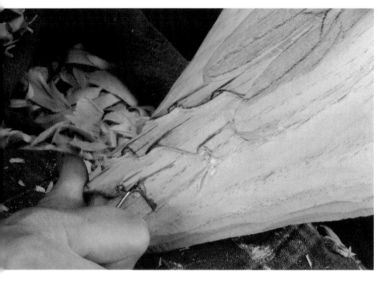

Score down the fold line.

Slice up beside the score line to tuck the fold under.

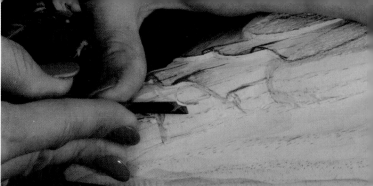

Round the edge of the fold.

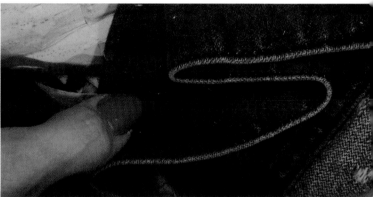

The fold is like this.

I've created this edge...

and now I need to create this area of return.

Score the upper line...

and come back to it with a chisel to drop the return back a little bit.

Clean up the return with a knife.

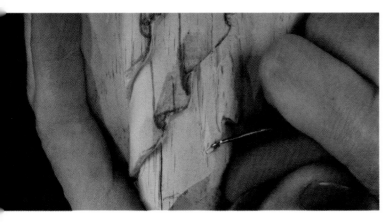

Repeat at each of the linen folds.

Scoop out the underside of the returns with a very small gouge to give them depth.

The first segment done.

Work your way up the gown doing one segment at a time.

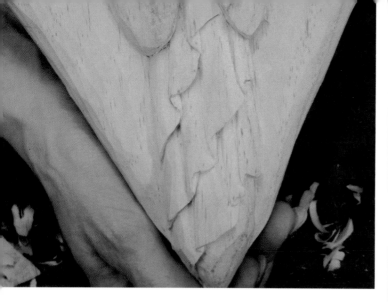

The completed folds.

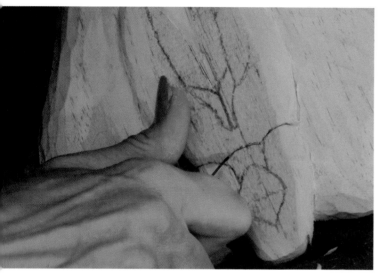

To bring the arms and hands out I need to drop the shoulders back. Begin by scoring the hairline and the neck line of the gown.

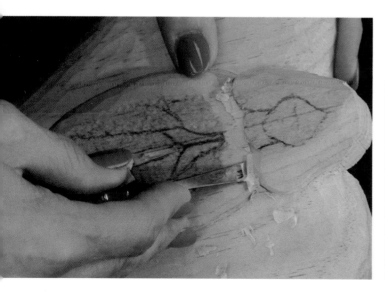

Trim the upper body back to the score line.

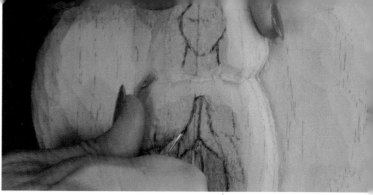

Next score around the hands.

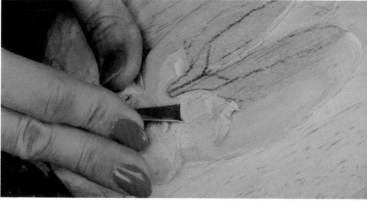

Reduce the body beside the hands.

Rescore and deepen the upper body surface.

Continue to drop the chest back.

Score the bottom edge of the hands and the line of the sleeve opening.

Clean out the opening of the sleeve.

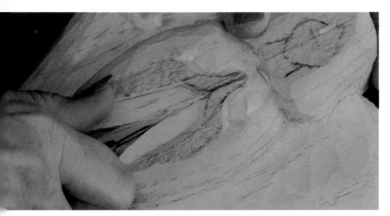

At the point where the sleeves meet I've come down to the level of the gown. I need to deepen the space between the sleeves.

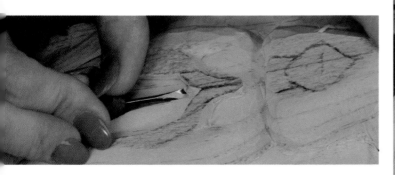

After scoring the lines, I clean the area out with a micro skew chisel.

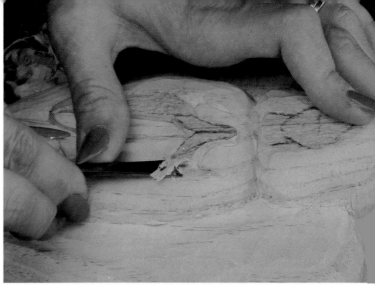

Clean up the sleeve.

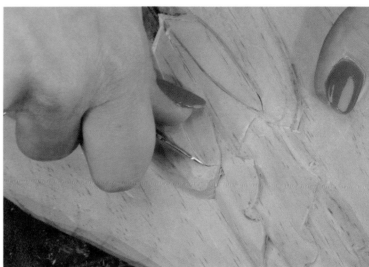

To accentuate the opening at the bottom of the sleeve, score the line...

and clean it out with a chisel.

The sleeve on your left is finished while the one on the right has yet to be carved. You can see how flat it appears.

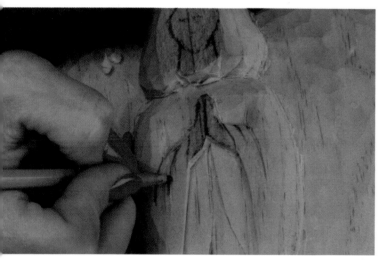

Draw in a couple of wrinkles on the forearm of the sleeve.

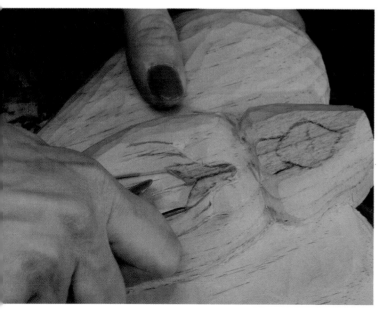

Score the opening of the sleeve on the wrist.

Shape the wrist and hand.

Seperate the hands with the v-tool.

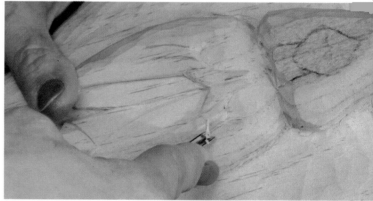

Use the v-tool to define the wrinkles in the forearm of the sleeve.

Soften the wrinkles by rounding their edges with a chisel.

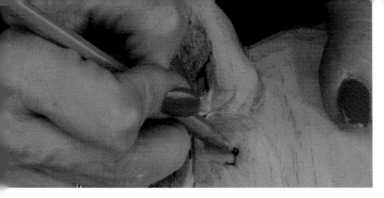

I want to deepen this corner to create more definition.

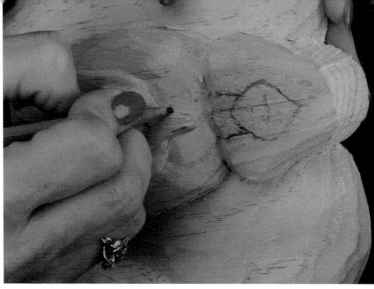

Draw in some fingers. I'm not sure if I want them, and drawing helps me see.

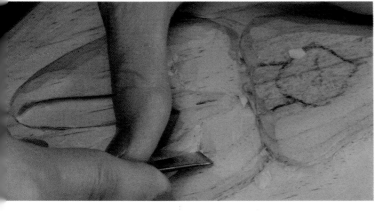

Use a chisel to clean it out.

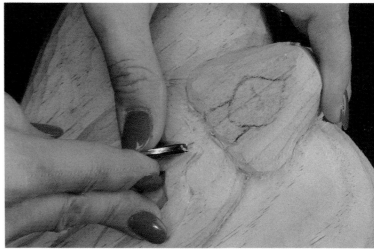

I like them, so I am going to make a shallow v-tool cut to define the fingers.

Repeat on the other side.

Slightly soften the line between the hands with the chisel.

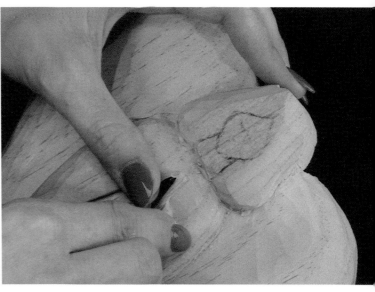

With the tip of the knife I soften the fingers just a little bit.

Shorten the pinky finger by removing the wood above it.

The wrist is a little thick and needs shaping. I'm using a skew for this.

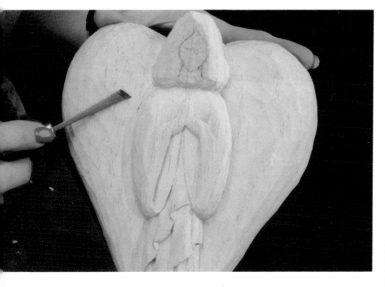

Progress. As I look at it, I think I need to drop the wings back even more to bring out the body.

Score around the body.

A slice along the body with a chisel.

Shape the top of the head.

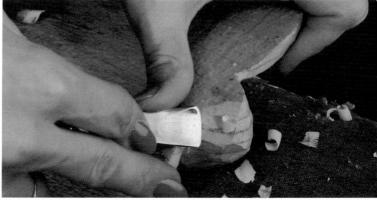

Round the back of the head forward,

16

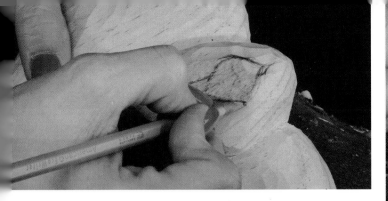

Redraw the lines of the face.

The faces are the hardest part. Begin by scoring the lines of the neck and the outline of the face.

Trim the outside of the face back to the score line.

Start under the chin and shape the neck back a little bit.

Round over the surface of the face...

taking it to this point.

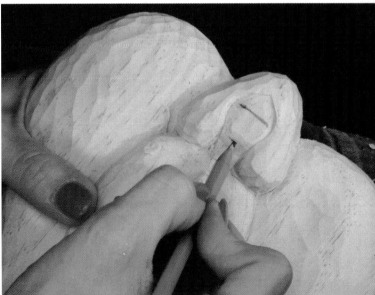

Draw the line of the eyes and define the bottom of the chin.

17

Halfway between mark the line of the bottom of the nose.

Score across the eye line.

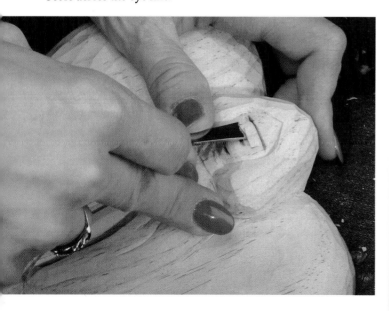

From the end of the nose, cut a wedge back to the eye line, all the way across the face.

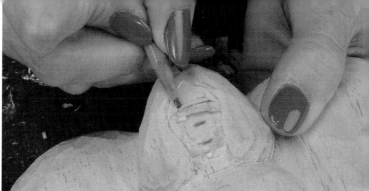

Draw a brow line just above the eye line.

From the brow line cut a wedge back to the eye line.

The result is a depression for the eyes.

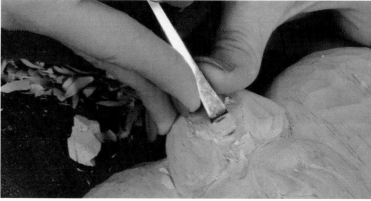

Cut straight in under the nose...

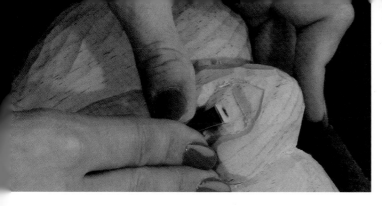

and make a wedge cut back along the upper lip.

Progress.

Draw in the sides of the nose. It is really big for now, but will be reduced as I refine it and add details.

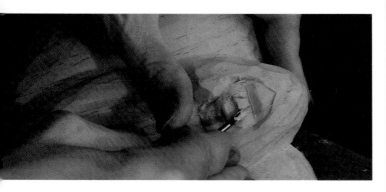

With a micro gouge cut a line starting close to the chin and up the side of the nose.

Do the same on the other side for this result.

I want to see more of her face, so I am going to remove some of the hair to open it up.

The result.

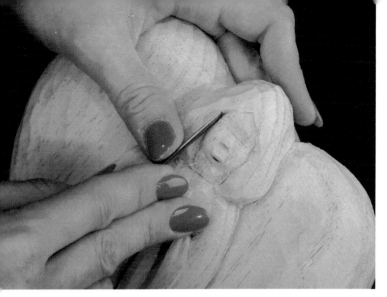

I run the chisel straight up beside the eyes to create the temporal plane.

Halfway between the bridge of the nose and the bottom of the nose is the cheek bone.

From the cheek bone I cut done at an angle toward the chin, creating the plane of the jaw.

The result.

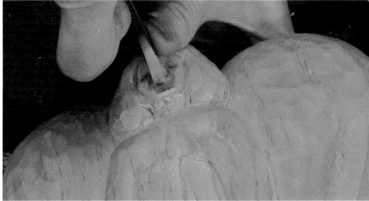

Press the chisel straight in on the chin line to create more of a chin.

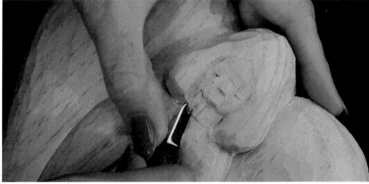

Clean up the neck a little, deepening the line as it goes beneath the hair.

Progress.

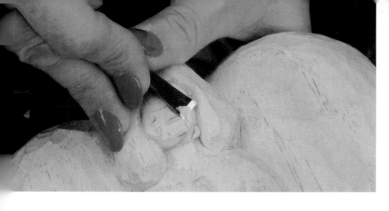

Drop the surface of the cheek back to bring out the nose.

Round the bottom surface of the nose.

Progress.

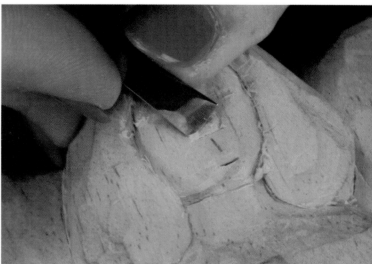

Draw a line down the center of the nose and mouth.

Knock off the corner of the nose.

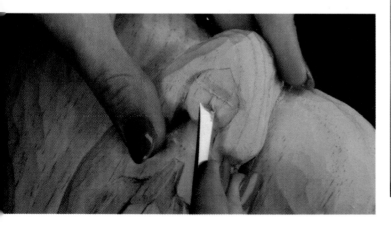

Shape the nose so the highest point is down the center.

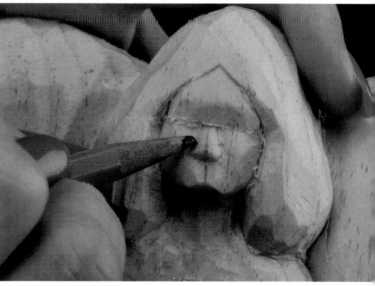

Make a dot at the end of the nose and one at the top of each nostril flange, where it meets the face.

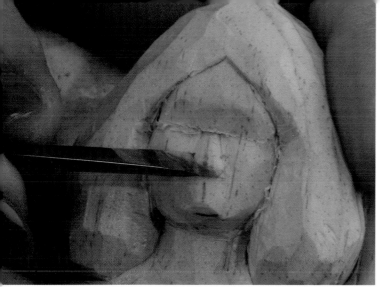

Align the blade of the chisel between the dots...

Repeat on the other side for this result.

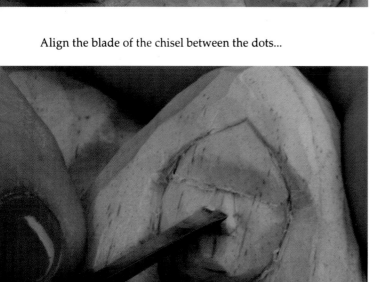

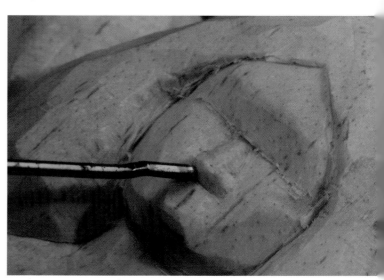

and cut in and up in a scooping cut.

Create the nostril by pushing in with micro gouge, keeping the cup side down.

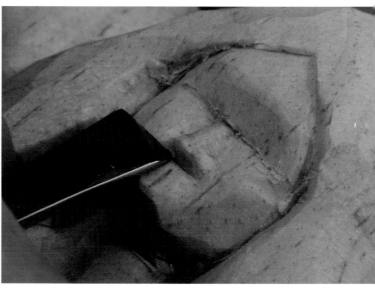

This defines the flange of the nostril

Clip off the waste with the corner of the chisel.

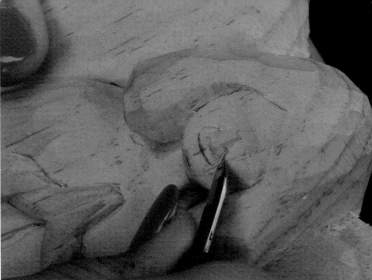

Before finishing the nose I need to establish the line of the mouth. The line between the lips is 1/3 of the distance from the nose to the chin.

Trim back to this line, following the surface of the cheek.

Smile lines run from the top of the nostril flange to the corner of the mouth.

This creates the smile line.

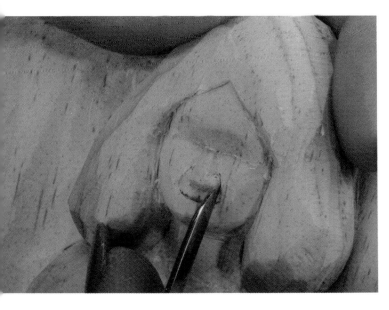

Cut straight into the cheek around the nostril flange.

With the smile lines established...

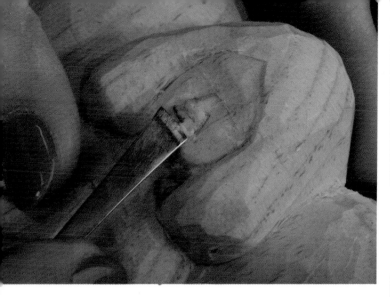

I need to round the area of the mouth. The center of the mouth should be the high point.

Redraw the line between the lips. Notice how it dips slightly in the center.

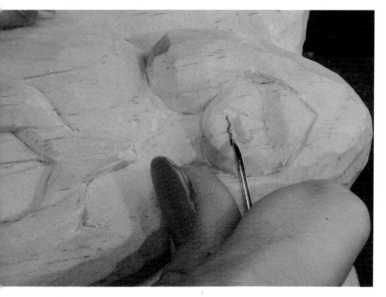

Score the line between the lips.

Place the point of the knife in the corner of the mouth, and with a paper cutter motion, cut along the surface of the lip back to the middle.

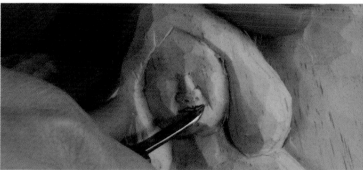

Do the same from the other corner.

Do the same for the top lip, from one side...

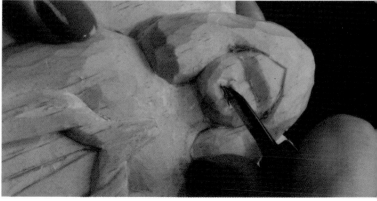

and the other.

These five cuts form the mouth.

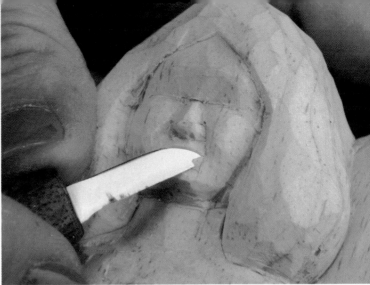

The lower lip tucks under the upper, so clip off the outside corners of the lower lip.

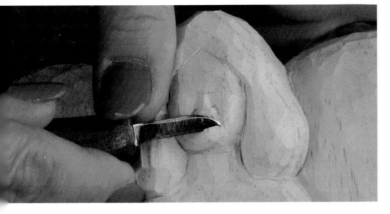

To bring the mouth out from the chin, slice down below the lip...

and come back to the first cut with a scooping cut from the chin. Do one side then the other.

The mouth is basically finished.

Progress on the mouth.

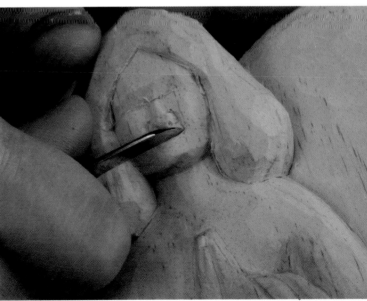

Score the mouth into the corners to create a smile.

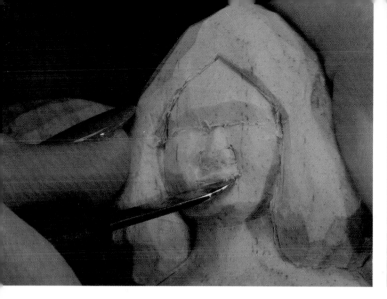

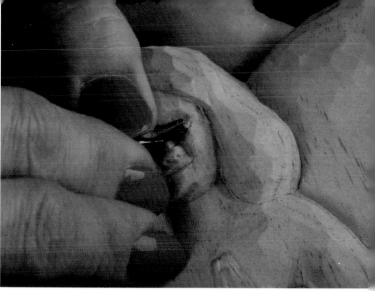

Clip the bottom lip back to the score line.

and below the eye.

Draw in the area of the eyes which will be deepened.

This leaves a small eye mound in the center.

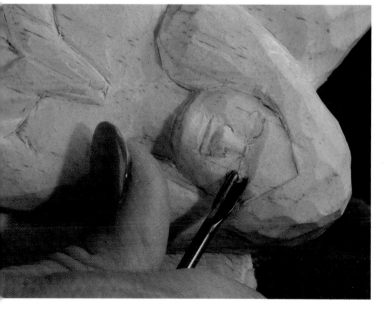

With a small gouge scoop above...

Draw a line through the center of the eye, then make a dot at the end of the opening at either side, and another at the top of the opening.

26

Connect the dots to establish the shape of the eye.

Do the same on the bottom line.

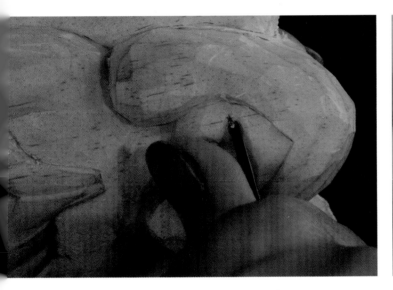

With the micro v-tool follow the line from the top of the arch into the corner going one way....

Before going further do the other eye. To keep symmetry, it is important to repeat each phase of the eye on the other side before proceeding.

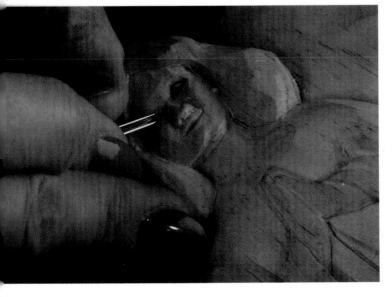

then the other.

With the knife as flat as possible, flatten the eyeball.

Repeat on the other side.

On the lines of the eye, press straight down into the corners.

Reach in with the point of the knife and clip the corner out.

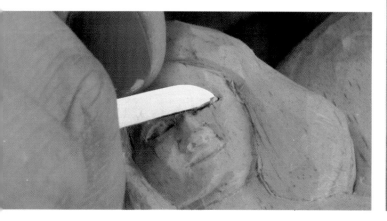

Repeat on the other eye.

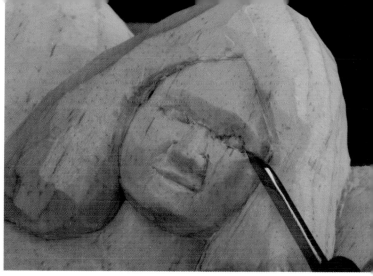

Check the eye for symmetry and adjust as needed. When that is done, follow the line of the upper lid and carry a score line past the corner of the eye.

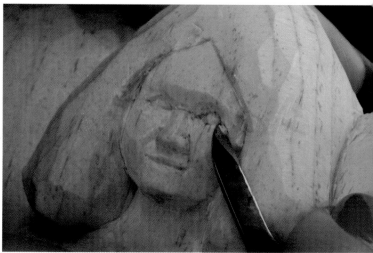

Cut back to the score line along the surface of the lower lid to tuck it under the upper lid. This is just like I did with the lower lip.

Progress on the eyes.

With a micro v-tool, start at the center of the eyelid and eyelid crease line.

The result.

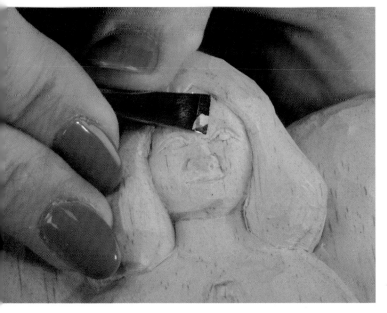

Soften the hard ridge at the center of the brow.

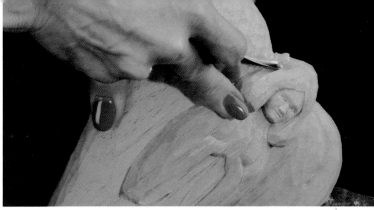

A large gouge sets the major flow lines of the hair.

A part down the middle finishes the major flows.

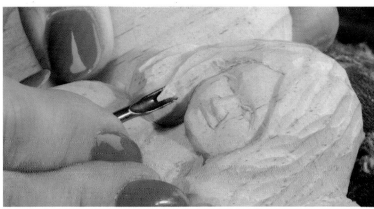

The texturing is done with a smaller gouge.

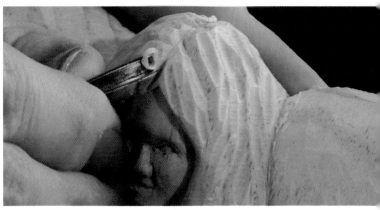

A v-tool is the final step in carving the hair.

You may need to make some adjustments after carving the hair. Here the bangs have created the need to deepen the forehead. I scored the edges and carve it with a straight chisel.

Draw in the neck line and score it.

The carving on the face is finished.

Trim back to the score line from the neck.

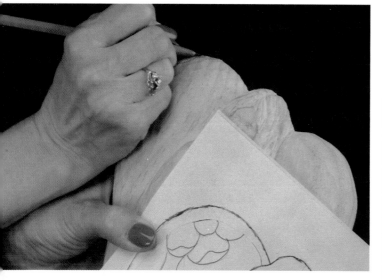

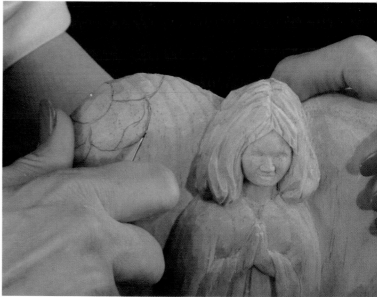

Transfer the pattern for the wings from the pattern. You can do this with carbon paper, or, as I find easier, just eyeball it and draw it freehand.

Score around the flowers and foliage on the right wing.

30

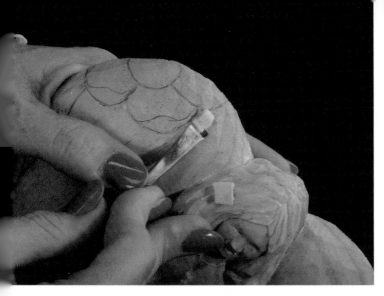

Relieve the area around the flower using a chisel.

Score the lines between the petals of the flowers in preparation for layering.

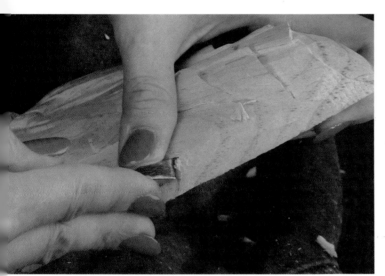

Round over the raised edge of the design.

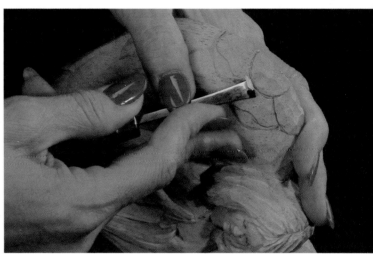

By slicing along the edge of the lower petal, tuck the center petal under it...

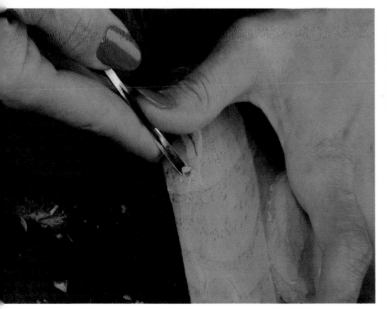

Use a v-tool to separate the bottom leaf from the stem.

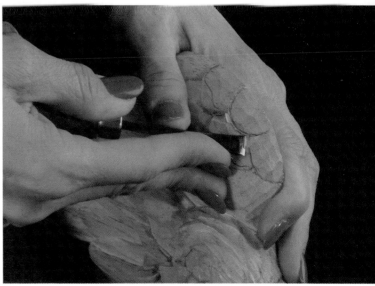

and under the flower's center.

Tuck the upper petal under the center one in the same way.

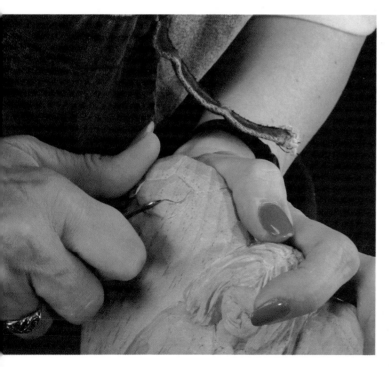

The lower two petals curl back on themselves. Score a line in the curl...

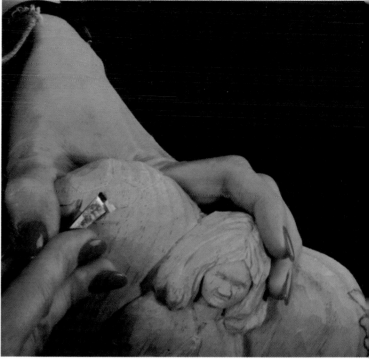

and slice along it from the inside of the petal.

One side done.

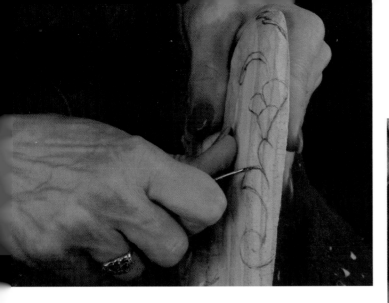

Use the same techniques to carve the foliage on the other wing.

The bottom of the gown seems unfinished, so I will add one more tier of folds.

This gives it a much more refined look.

Use a gouge to clean the back of the piece and give it some texture. It feels better and is a much more professional way of doing things.

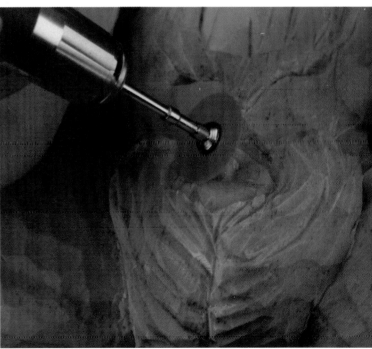

Before painting I sand the large surfaces of the face with a rotary tool sanding wheel, using a fine grit.

Painting the Angel

I use hobby acrylics, which are available under
a variety of names at most craft stores.

Color Palette

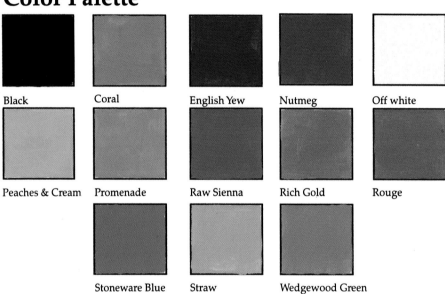

Black   Coral   English Yew   Nutmeg   Off white

Peaches & Cream   Promenade   Raw Sienna   Rich Gold   Rouge

Stoneware Blue   Straw   Wedgewood Green

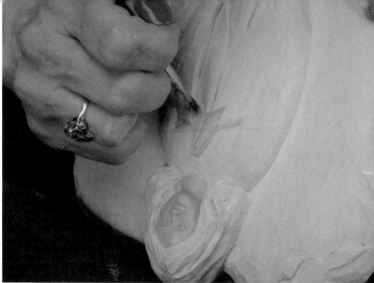

The base coat is an off-white. Over a palette pad I place a damp paper towel. I pour my paints on this so they will stay wet longer.

Use the same color on the hands.

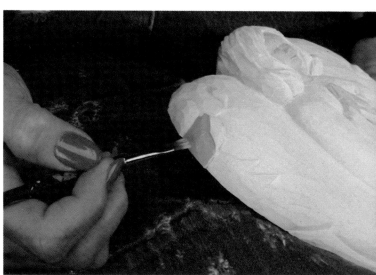

Cover the entire piece with a thin coat of off-white paint.

The flower petals are painted Promenade.

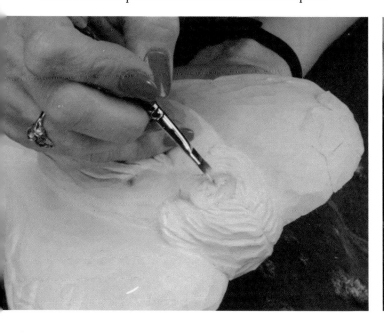

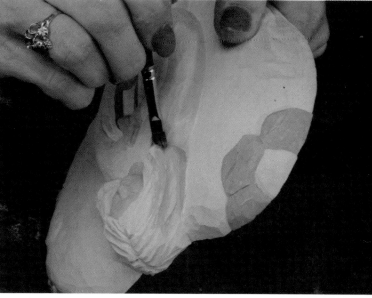

Apply a base coat of flesh to the face.

The Straw paint produces a nice yellow hair.

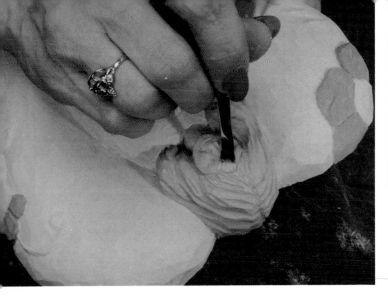

Apply a second coat of flesh to the face and hands. There will be three coats in all. If the hands and face are not painted well, the antiquing process will leave them looking dirty.

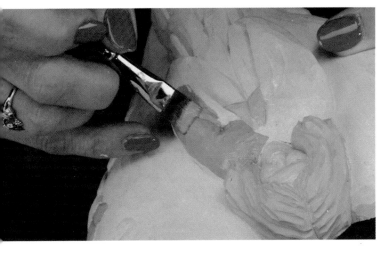

Apply Wedgewood Green to the gown...

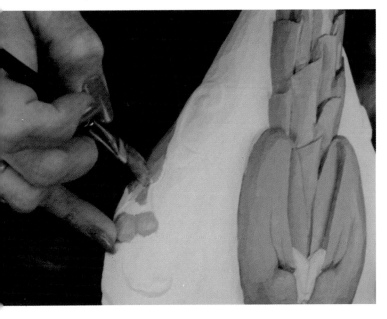

and the foliage.

Apply yellow to the center of the flower.

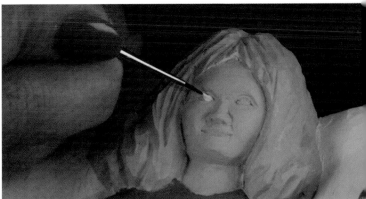

Apply the off white paint to the eyeball.

A drop of blue makes the iris.

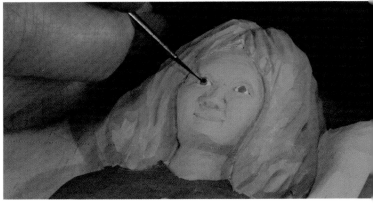

A touch of black is used for the pupil.

With a very fine brush use dark brown paint to line the eye.

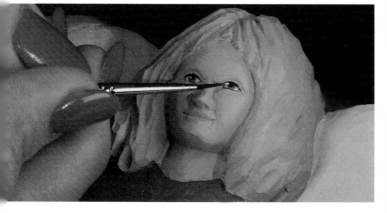

As a finishing touch I add a glint of white paint to each eye to give it life. The dots should be in the same position in both.

The finished eye.

Add Rouge to the lips.

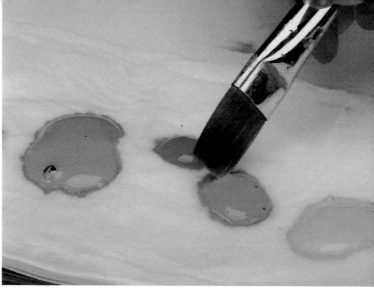

The color in the cheeks begins with a coat of Coral. I corner load my brush by dipping one corner in the paint...

and working it into the brush on the palette paper. This should give a gradation of paint in the brush, moving from strong pigment on the corner to no pigment toward the middle.

With the loaded corner of the brush toward the middle of the cheek, add some color.

The result.

Corner load your brush with a mixture of flesh and brown, and use it to shade the wrist. Keep the loaded part of the brush near the sleeve.

When the Coral color has dried, corner load your brush with the brighter Rouge and apply it over the coral. While this will make our angel look more like a call girl for now, the antiquing process will soften the color. When you are antiquing you need to begin with bright colors.

Corner load the brush with Rouge and shade the petals of the flowers.

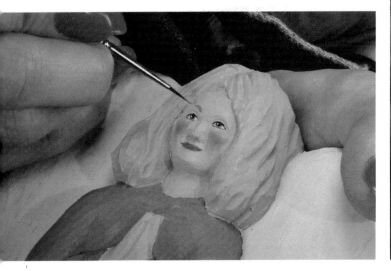

With light brown on a fine brush, add some eyebrows.

Continue the shading under the turned tip of the petal.

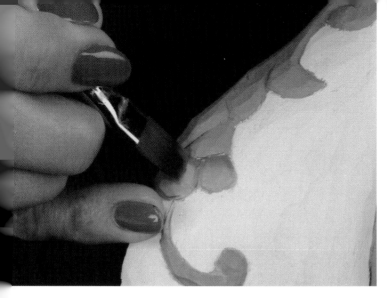

Do the same on the bud.

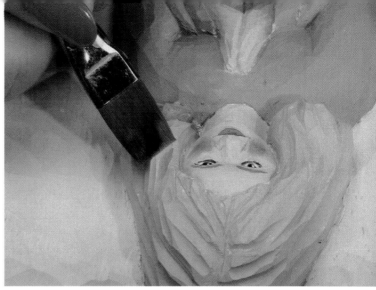

With the same color shade the hair taking the darker tones into the deeper areas.

Corner load your brush with flesh, and highlight the turned up end of the petal.

Pick up the high points of the hair with the off white paint.

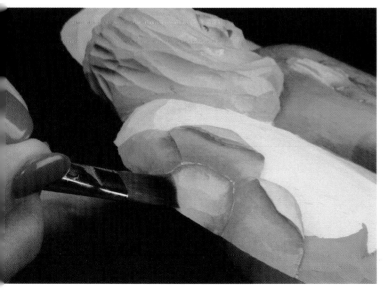

Corner load the brush with raw sienna and shade around the center of the flower.

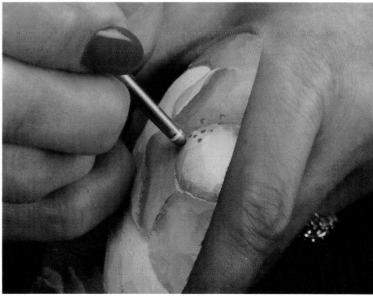

Load the handle end of a brush with medium brown paint and lightly touch it to the flower blossom to make dots.

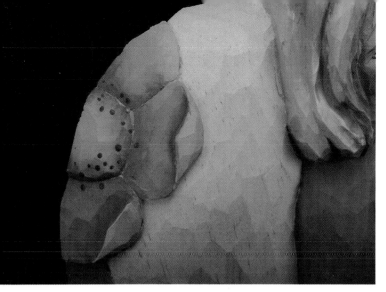

The result.

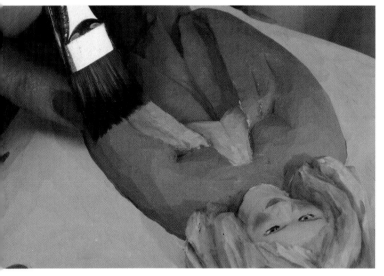

A mixture of light green with a touch of yellow for warmth, is used to highlight the gown. Corner load it into a larger brush, and apply it to the sleeves...

the shoulders...

the fabric folds...

and the foliage.

The highlighting complete.

40

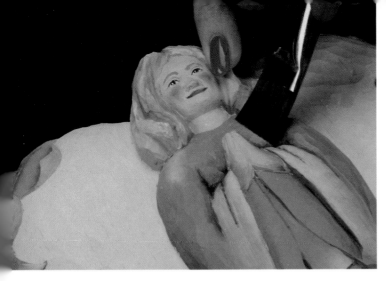

Now with a English Yew green on a corner loaded brush add some shading to the gown behind the hands...

under the tiers of the gown...

inside the sleeve...

and foliage.

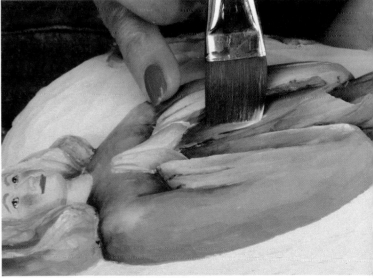

a little bit under the hair...

The inside of the sleeve needs a little highlight on the edge, using the lighter green color.

Warm gold is applied as a trim around the neck...

Sign it and it's ready to antique.

at the edge of the sleeve opening...

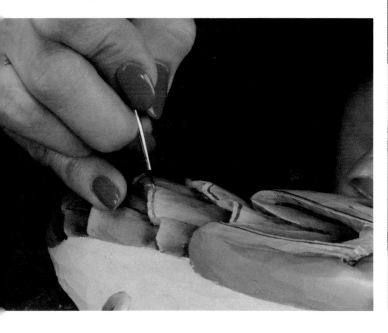

and along the edges of the tiers.

Spray with at least four coats of a fast drying spray varnish.

The antiquing is done with burnt umber artist's oils mixed with thinner to a consistency of melted chocolate chips.

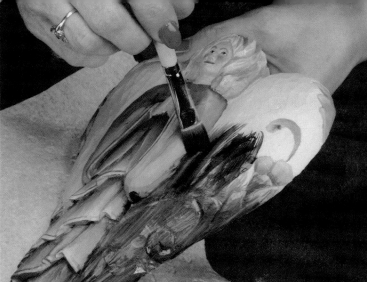

When you are satisfied with the test, cover the whole piece with the burnt umber paint.

Test coat a corner to be sure the paint is compatible with the oil finish.

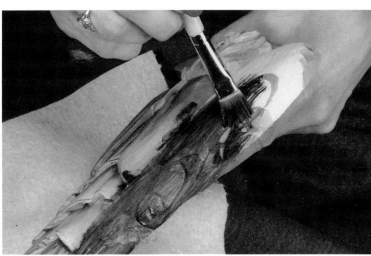

Be sure to get in the folds and crevices of the carving.

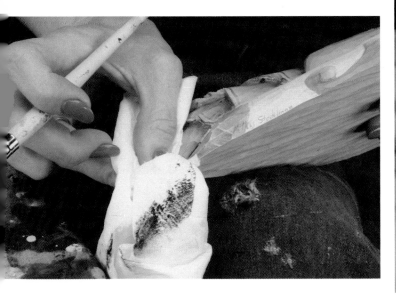

Wipe it off immediately. This paint is grabbing more than I want, so I will dilute it more.

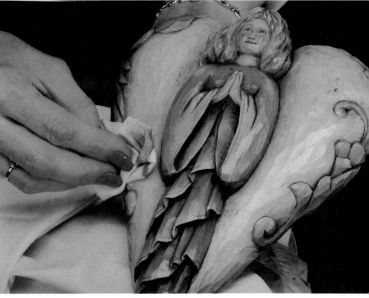

Wipe the brown away immediately with a dry cloth.

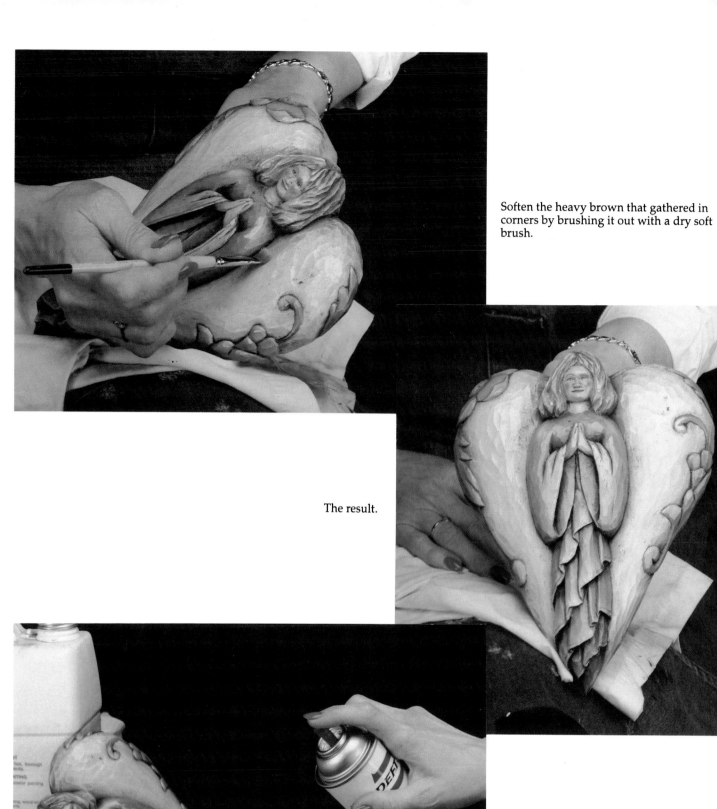

Soften the heavy brown that gathered in corners by brushing it out with a dry soft brush.

The result.

Allow the paint to dry for 48 hours then add a light coat of wood finish spray.

The Gallery
and Patterns

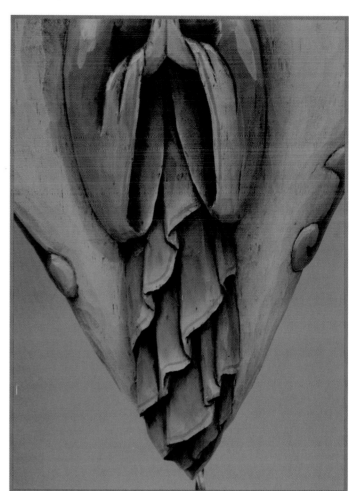

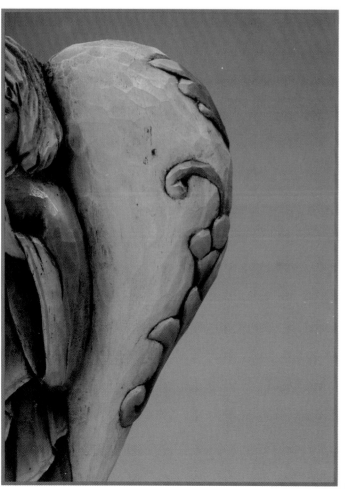

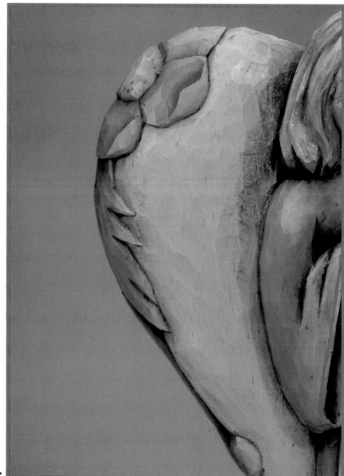

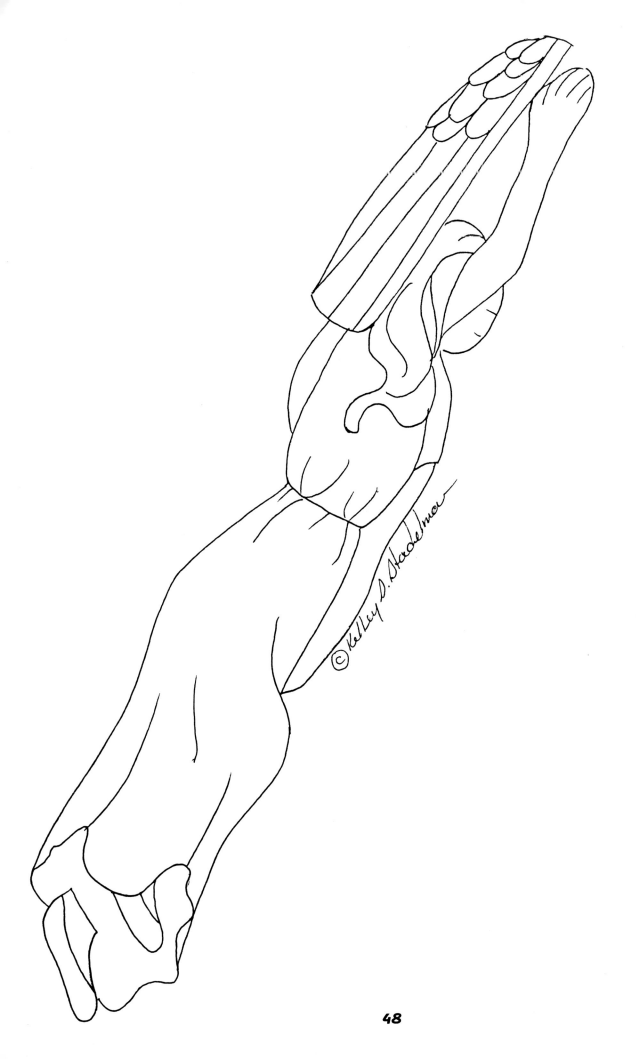

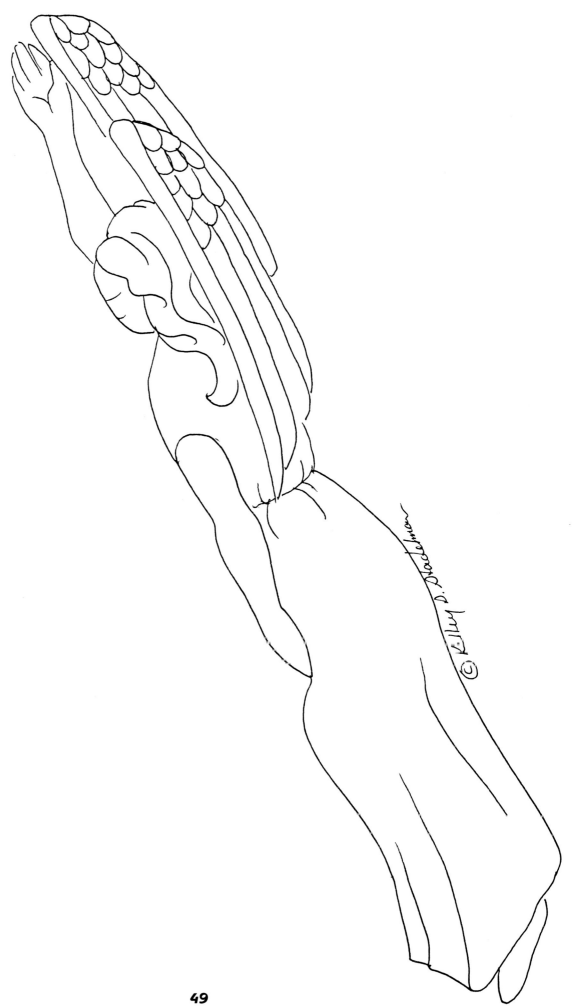

50

© Kelley D. Stadelman

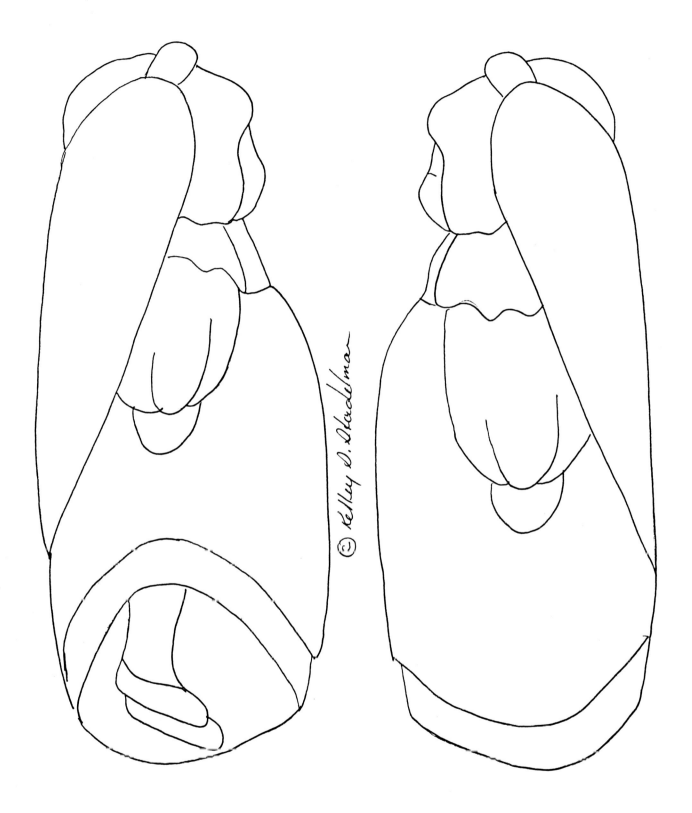

©Kelley D. Noelohn

©Kelley D. Noelohn

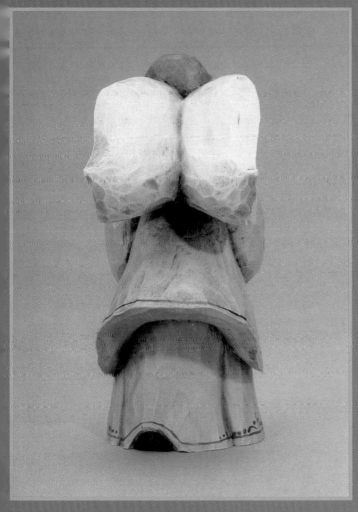

© Kelley S. Blackman

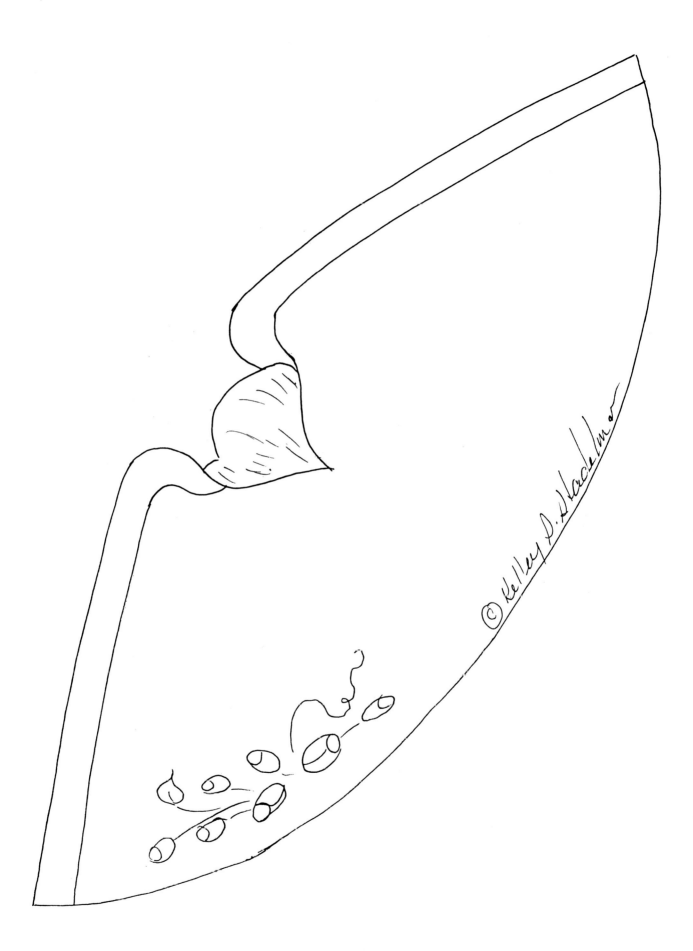